The Project Method: The Use Of The Purposeful Act In The Educative Process

William Heard Kilpatrick

THE PROJECT METHOD

The Use of the Purposeful Act
in the Educative Process

By

William Heard Kilpatrick

Professor of Education, Teachers College
Columbia University

Eleventh Impression
March, 1929

Published by
Teachers College, Columbia University
525 West 120th Street
New York City

5 DH-3-29

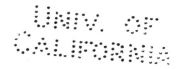

THE PROJECT METHOD [1]

The word 'project' is perhaps the latest arrival to knock for admittance at the door of educational terminology. Shall we admit the stranger? Not wisely unless two preliminary questions have first been answered in the affirmative: First, is there behind the proposed term and waiting even now to be christened a valid notion or concept which promises to render appreciable service in educational thinking? Second, if we grant the foregoing, does the term 'project' fitly designate the waiting concept? Because the question as to the concept and its worth is so much more significant than any matter of mere names, this discussion will deal almost exclusively with the first of the two inquiries. It is indeed entirely possible that some other term, as 'purposeful act', for example, would call attention to a more important element in the concept, and, if so, might prove superior as a term to the word 'project'. At the outset it is probably wise to caution the reader against expecting any great amount of novelty in the idea here presented. The metaphor of christening is not to be taken too seriously; the concept to be considered is not in fact newly born. Not a few readers will be disappointed that after all so little new is presented.

A little of the personal may perhaps serve to introduce the more formal discussion. In attacking with successive classes in educational theory the problem of method, I had felt increasingly the need of unifying more completely a number of important related aspects of the educative process. I began to hope for some one concept which might serve this end. Such a concept, if found, must, so I thought, emphasize the factor of action, preferably wholehearted vigorous activity. It must at the same time provide a place for the adequate utilization of the laws of learning, and no less for the essential elements of the ethical quality of conduct. The last named looks of course to the social situation as well as to the individual attitude. Along with these should go, as it seemed, the important generalization that edu-

[1] Reprinted from TEACHERS COLLEGE RECORD, Vol. XIX, No. 4 (September, 1918). Copyright 1918.

cation is life—so easy to say and so hard to delimit. Could now
all of these be contemplated under one workable notion? If yes
a great gain. In proportion as such a unifying concept could b
found, in like proportion would the work of presenting educationa
theory be facilitated; in the same proportion should be the rapi
spread of a better practice.

But could this unifying idea be found? Here was in fact the age
old problem of effective logical organization. My whole philosophi
outlook had made me suspicious of so-called 'fundamental principles'
Was there yet another way of attaining unity? I do not mean to
say that I asked these questions, either in these words or in thi
order. Rather is this a retrospective ordering of the more importan
outcomes. As the desired unification lay specifically in the field
of method, might not some typical unit of concrete procedure suppl
the need—some unit of conduct that should be, as it were, a sampl
of life, a fair sample of the worthy life and consequently of education.
As these questionings rose more definitely to mind, there came
increasingly a belief—corroborated on many sides—that the unifying
idea I sought was to be found in the conception of wholehearted
purposeful activity proceeding in a social environment, or more
briefly, in the unit element of such activity, the hearty purposeful
act.

It is to this purposeful act with the emphasis on the word purpose
that I myself apply the term 'project'. I did not invent the term
nor did I start it on its educational career. Indeed, I do not know
how long it had already been in use. I did, however, consciously
appropriate the word to designate to myself and for my classes the
typical unit of the worthy life described above. Others who were
using the term seemed to me either to use it in a mechanical and
partial sense or to be intending in a general way what I tried to
define more exactly. The purpose of this article is to attempt to
clarify the concept underlying the term as much as it is to defend the
claim of the concept to a place in our educational thinking. The
actual terminology with which to designate the concept is, as was
said before, to my mind a matter of relatively small moment. If,
however, we think of a project as a pro-ject, something pro-jected,
the reason for adopting the term may better appear.

Postponing yet a little further the more systematic presenta-
tion of the matter, let us from some typical instances see more

concretely what is contemplated under the term project or hearty purposeful act. Suppose a girl has made a dress. If she did in hearty fashion purpose to make the dress, if she planned it, if she made it herself, then I should say the instance is that of a typical project. We have in it a wholehearted purposeful act carried on amid social surroundings. That the dressmaking was purposeful is clear; and the purpose once formed dominated each succeeding step in the process and gave unity to the whole. That the girl was wholehearted in the work was assured in the illustration. That the activity proceeded in a social environment is clear; other girls at least are to see the dress. As another instance, suppose a boy undertakes to get out a school newspaper. If he is in earnest about it, we again have an effective purpose as the essence of a project. So we may instance a pupil writing a letter (if the hearty purpose is present), a child listening absorbedly to a story, Newton explaining the motion of the moon on the principles of terrestrial dynamics, Demosthenes trying to arouse the Greeks against Philip, Da Vinci painting the *Last Supper*, my writing this article, a boy solving with felt purpose an 'original' in geometry. All of the foregoing have been acts of individual purposing, but there are just as truly group projects: a class presents a play, a group of boys organize a baseball nine, three pupils prepare to read a story to their comrades. It is clear then that projects may present every variety that purposes present in life. It is also clear that a mere description of outwardly observable facts might not disclose the essential factor, namely the presence of a dominating purpose. It is equally true that there can be every degree of approximation to full projects according as the animating purpose varies in clearness and strength. If we conceive activities as ranging on a scale from those performed under dire compulsion up to those into which one puts his 'whole heart', the argument herein made restricts the term 'project' or purposeful act to the upper portions of the scale. An exact dividing line is hard to draw, and yields indeed in importance to the notion that psychological value increases with the degree of approximation to 'wholeheartedness'. As to the social environment element, some may feel that, however important this is to the fullest educative experience, it is still not essential to the conception of the purposeful act as here presented. These might, therefore, wish to leave this element out of the defining discussion. To this I should not object if it were clearly understood that the resulting concept—now essentially psychological in character—demands, generally speaking, the social situation both for its practical working and for the comparative valuation of proffered projects.

With this general introduction, we may, in the first place, say that the purposeful act is the typical unit of the worthy life. Not that all purposes are good, but that the worthy life consists of purposive activity and not mere drifting. We scorn the man who passively accepts what 'fate' or mere chance brings to him. We admire the man who is master of his fate, who with deliberate regard for a total situation forms clear and far-reaching purposes, who plans and executes with nice care the purposes so formed. A man who habitually so regulates his life with reference to worthy social aims meets at once the demands for practical efficiency and of moral responsibility. Such a one presents the ideal of democratic citizenship. It is equally true that the purposeful act is not the unit of life for the serf or the slave. These poor unfortunates must in the interest of the overmastering system be habituated to act with a minimum of their own purposing and with a maximum of servile acceptance of others' purposes. In important matters they merely follow plans handed down to them from above, and execute these according to prescribed directions. For them another carries responsibility and upon the results of their labor another passes judgment. No such plan as that here advocated would produce the kind of docility required for their hopeless fate. But it is a democracy which we contemplate and with which we are here concerned

As the purposeful act is thus the typical unit of the worthy life in a democratic society, so also should it be made the typical unit of school procedure. We of America have for years increasingly desired that education be considered as life itself and not as a mere preparation for later living. The conception before us promises a definite step toward the attainment of this end. If the purposeful act be in reality the typical unit of the worthy life, then it follows that to base education on purposeful acts is exactly to identify the process of education with worthy living itself. The two become then the same. All the arguments for placing education on a life basis seem, to me at any rate, to concur in support of this thesis. On this basis education has become life. And if the purposeful act thus makes of education life itself, could we reasoning in

w essen·
ing, the
·mpara·

ce, say
:. Not
of pur·
to pas·
idmire
l for a
plans
i who
aims
noral
izen·
iit of
i the
th a
rvile
rely
iese
ion·
ent.
of
ich

in
iit
·ly
a
n·
ie
,
y
e
i
i

advance expect to find a better preparation for later life than practice in living now? We have heard of old that "we learn to do by doing," and much wisdom resides in the saying. If the worthy life of the coming day is to consist of well-chosen purposeful acts, what preparation for that time could promise more than practice now, under discriminating guidance, in forming and executing worthy purposes? To this end must the child have within rather large limits the opportunity to purpose. For the issues of his act he must —in like limits—be held accountable. That the child may properly progress, the total situation—all the factors of life, including comrades—speaking, if need be through the teacher, must make clear its selective judgment upon what is done, approving the better, rejecting the worse. In a true sense the whole remaining discussion is but to support the contention here argued in advance that education based on the purposeful act prepares best for life while at the same time it constitutes the present worthy life itself.

A more explicit reason for making the purposeful act the typical unit of instruction is found in the utilization of the laws of learning which this plan affords. I am assuming that it is not necessary in this paper to justify or even explain at length these laws.[2] Any act of conduct consists of a response to the existing situation. That response in preference to any other followed the given situation because there existed in the nervous system a bond or connection joining the stimulus of that situation with that response. Some such bonds come with us into the world, as, for example, the infant cries (responds) when he is very hungry (situation acting as stimulus). Other bonds are acquired, as when the hungry child later asks in words for food. The process of acquiring or otherwise changing bonds we call learning. The careful statements of the conditions under which bonds are built or changed are the laws of learning. Bonds are not always equally *ready* to act: when I am angry, the bonds that have to do with smiling are distinctly unready; other bonds controlling uglier behavior are quite ready. When a bond is ready to act, to act gives *satisfaction* and not to act gives *annoyance*. When a bond is not ready to act, to act gives annoyance and not to act gives satisfaction. These two statements constitute the law of Readiness. The law that most concerns us in this discussion is that

[2] The discussion which here follows is adapted from Thorndike's *Educational Psychology*, Vol. II, pp. 1-16.

of Effect: when a modifiable bond acts, it is strengthened or weakened according as satisfaction or annoyance results. The ordinary psychology of common observation has not been so conscious of these two laws as it has of the third law, that of Exercise; but for our present purposes, repetition simply means the continued application of the law of Effect.[1] There are yet other laws necessary for a full explanation of the facts of learning. Our available space allows for only one more, that of 'set' or attitude, the others we have to assume without explicit reference. When a person is very angry, he is sometimes colloquially said to be "mad all over." Such a phrase implies that many bonds are ready to act conjointly to an end, in this case, the end of overcoming or doing damage to the object of anger. Under such conditions there is (a) available and at work a stock of energy for attaining the end, (b) a state of readiness in the bonds pertaining to the activity at hand, and (c) a correlative unreadiness on the part of the bonds that might thwart the attainment of the end contemplated by the 'set.' The reader is asked to note (a) how a 'set' towards an end means readiness in and action of pertinent bonds with reference to that end, (b) how this end defines success, (c) how readiness in the bonds means satisfaction when success is attained, and (d) how satisfaction strengthens the bonds whose action brought success. These facts fit well with the generalization that man's mental powers and capacities came into being in connection with the continual attaining of ends demanded by the life of the organism. The capacity for 'set' means in the case of man the capacity for persistent and directed action. Such action means for our discussion not only that (objective) success is more likely to result, but that learning inheres in the process. The bonds whose action brought success are by the resulting satisfaction more firmly fixed, both as distinct bonds separately considered and as a system of bonds working together under the 'set'. Set, readiness, persistent action, success, satisfaction, and learning are inherently connected.

How then does the purposeful act utilize the laws of learning? A boy is intent upon making a kite that will fly. Hitherto he has not succeeded. His purpose is clear. This purpose is but the 'set' consciously and volitionally bent on its end. As set the pur-

[1] The law of Exercise does of course include more than this, as the successful educator must know if he would meet all situations.

pose is the inner urge that carries the boy on in the face of hindrance and difficulty. It brings 'readiness' to pertinent inner resources of knowledge and thought. Eye and hand are made alert. The purpose acting as aim guides the boy's thinking, directs his examination of plan and material, elicits from within appropriate suggestions, and tests these several suggestions by their pertinency to the end in view. The purpose in that it contemplates a specific end defines success: the kite must fly or he has failed. The progressive attaining of success with reference to subordinate aims brings satisfaction at the successive stages of completion. Satisfaction in detail and in respect of the whole by the automatic working of the second law of learning (Effect) fixes the several bonds which by their successive successes brought the finally successful kite. The purpose thus supplies the motive power, makes available inner resources, guides the process to its preconceived end, and by this satisfying success fixes in the boy's mind and character the successful steps as part and parcel of one whole. The purposeful act does utilize the laws of learning.

But this account does not yet exhaust the influence of the purpose on the resulting learning. Suppose as extreme cases two boys making kites, the one with wholeheartedness of purpose, as we have just described, the other under direct compulsion as a most unwelcome task. For simplicity's sake suppose the latter under enforced directions makes a kite identical with the other. The steps that in either case actually produced the kite let us call the *primary* responses for that case. Evidently these will, in the two cases, in part agree, and in part differ. The respects in which they agree furnish the kind of responses that we can and customarily do assign as tasks—the external irreducible minimum for the matter at hand. Upon such we can feasibly insist, even to the point of punishment if we do so decide. Additional to the primary responses which produced the respective kites, there will be yet other responses that accompany the kitemaking, not so much by way of outward doing as of inward thought and feeling. These additional responses may be divided into *associate* and *concomitant* responses. By associate responses we refer to those thoughts which are suggested in rather close connection with the primary responses and with the materials used and the

ends sought.[4] By the term concomitant reference is made to certain
responses yet a little further off from the immediate operation of
kitemaking, which result ultimately in attitudes and generalizations.
It is in this way that such attitudes are produced as self-respect or
the contrary, and such relatively abstract ideals as accuracy or
neatness. These words, primary, associate, and concomitant, will
be used as well of the resulting learning as of the responses that
bring the learning. The terminology is not entirely happy, and exact lines of division are not easy to draw; but the distinctions may
perhaps help us to see a further function of purpose.

As for the primary responses we need do little more than recall
the discussion of the immediately preceding paragraphs. The
factor of 'set' conditions the learning process. A strong set acting
through the satisfaction which attends success fixes quickly and
strongly the bonds which brought success. In the case of coercion,
however, a different state of affairs holds. There are in effect two
sets operating: one set, kept in existence solely through coercion,
is concerned to make a kite that will pass muster; the other set has
a different end and would pursue a different course were the coercion
removed. Each set in so far as it actually exists means a possible
satisfaction and in that degree a possible learning. But the two sets,
being opposed, mean at times a confusion as to the object of success;
and in every case each set destroys a part of the other's satisfaction
and so hampers the primary learning. Moreover, for the wholehearted act the several steps of the primary responses are welded
together, as it were, at the forge of conscious purpose, and so have
not only a stronger connection of part with part but greater flexi-
bility of the whole to thought. So far then as concerns even the
barest mechanics of kitemaking, the boy of wholehearted purpose
will emerge with a higher degree of skill and knowledge and his
learning will longer abide with him.

In the case of the associate responses, the difference is equally
noticeable. The unified set of wholeheartedness will render available all the pertinent connected inner resources. A wealth of mar-
ginal responses will be ready to come forward at every opportunity.
Thoughts will be turned over and over, and each step will be connected in many ways with other experiences. Alluring leads in

[4] The term accessory was used in the original article where the word associate is now used
with a slight difference of meaning, however.

various allied directions will open before the boy, which only the dominant present purpose could suffice to postpone. The element of satisfaction will attend connections seen, so that the complex of allied thinking will the longer remain as a mental possession. All of this is exactly not so with the other boy. The forbidden 'set', so long as it persists, will pretty effectually quench the glow of thought. Unreadiness will rather characterize his attitude. Responses accessory to the work at hand will be few in number, and the few that come will lack the element of satisfaction to fix them. Where the one boy has a wealth of associated ideas, the other has poverty. What abides with the one, is fleeting with the other. Even more pronounced is the difference in the by-products or concomitants from these contrasted activities. The one boy looks upon his school activity with joy and confidence and plans yet other projects; the other counts his school a bore and begins to look elsewhere for the expression there denied. To the one the teacher is a friend and comrade; to the other, a taskmaster and enemy. The one easily feels himself on the side of the school and other social agencies, the other with equal ease considers them all instruments of suppression. Furthermore, under the allied readiness which follows purpose, attention is more easily led to helpful generalizations of method and to such ideals as exactness or fairness. Desirable concomitants are more likely with the hearty purposeful act.

The contrasts here made are consciously of extremes. Most children live between the two. The question is whether we shall not consciously put before us as an ideal the one type of activity and approximate it as closely as we can rather than supinely rest content to live as close to the other type as do the general run of our American schools. Does not the ordinary school among us put its almost exclusive attention on the primary responses and the learning of these in the second fashion here described? Do we not too often reduce the subject matter of instruction to the level of this type alone? Does not our examination system—even our scientific tests at times—tend to carry us in the same direction? How many children at the close of a course decisively shut the book and say, "Thank gracious, I am through with that!" How many people 'get an education' and yet hate books and hate to think?

The thought suggested at the close of the preceding paragraph may be generalized into a criterion more widely applicable. The richness of life is seen upon reflection to depend, in large measure at least, upon the tendency of what one does to suggest and prepare for succeeding activities. Any activity—beyond the barest physical want—which does not thus 'lead on' becomes in time stale and flat. Such 'leading on' means that the individual has been modified so that he sees what before he did not see or does what before he could not do. But this is exactly to say that the activity has had an educative effect. Not to elaborate the argument, we may assert that the richness of life depends exactly on its tendency to lead one on to other like fruitful activity; that the degree of this tendency consists exactly in the educative effect of the activity involved; and that we may therefore take as the criterion of the value of any activity—whether intentionally educative or not—its tendency directly or indirectly to lead the individual and others whom he touches on to other like fruitful activity. If we apply this criterion to the common run of American schools we find exactly the discouraging results indicated above. It is the thesis of this paper that these evil results must inevitably follow the effort to found our educational procedure on an unending round of set tasks in conscious disregard of the element of dominant purpose in those who perform the tasks. This again is not to say that every purpose is good nor that the child is a suitable judge as between purposes nor that he is never to be forced to act against a purpose which he entertains. We contemplate no scheme of subordination of teacher or school to childish whim; but we do mean that any plan of educational procedure which does not aim consciously and insistently at securing and utilizing vigorous purposing on the part of the pupils is founded essentially on an ineffective and unfruitful basis. Nor is the quest for desirable purposes hopeless. There is no necessary conflict in kind between the social demands and the child's interests. Our whole fabric of institutional life grew out of human interests. The path of the race is here a possible path for the individual. There is no normal boy but has already many socially desirable interests and is capable of many more. It is the special duty and opportunity of the teacher to guide the pupil through his present interests and achievement into the wider interests and achievement demanded by the wider social life of the older world.

The question of moral education was implicitly raised in the preceding paragraph. What is the effect on morals of the plan herein advocated? A full discussion is unfortunately impossible. Speaking for myself, however, I consider the possibilities for building moral character in a régime of purposeful activity one of the strongest points in its favor; and contrariwise the tendency toward a selfish individualism one of the strongest counts against our customary set-task sit-alone-at-your-own-desk procedure. Moral character is primarily an affair of shared social relationships, the disposition to determine one's conduct and attitudes with reference to the welfare of the group. This means, psychologically, building stimulus-response bonds such that when certain ideas are present as stimuli certain approved responses will follow. We are then concerned that children get a goodly stock of ideas to serve as stimuli for conduct, that they develop good judgment for selecting the idea appropriate in a given case, and that they have firmly built such response bonds as will bring—as inevitably as possible—the appropriate conduct once the proper idea has been chosen. In terms of this (necessarily simplified) analysis we wish such school procedure as will most probably result in the requisite body of ideas, in the needed skill in judging a moral situation, and in unfailing appropriate response bonds. To get these three can we conceive of a better way than by living in a social *milieu* which provides, under competent supervision, for shared coping with a variety of social situations? In the school procedure here advocated children are living together in the pursuit of a rich variety of purposes, some individually sought, many conjointly. As must happen in social commingling, occasions of moral stress will arise, but here— fortunately—under conditions that exclude extreme and especially harmful cases. Under the eye of the skillful teacher the children as an embryonic society will make increasingly finer discriminations as to what is right and proper. Ideas and judgment come thus. Motive and occasion arise together; the teacher has but to steer the process of evaluating the situation. The teacher's success—if we believe in democracy—will consist in gradually eliminating himself or herself from the success of the procedure.

Not only do defined ideas and skill in judging come from such a situation, but response bonds as well. The continual sharing of purposes in such a school offers ideal conditions for forming the necessary habits of give and take. The laws of learning hold here as elsewhere, especially the law of Effect. If the child is to set up habits of acting, satisfaction must attend the doing or annoyance the failure. Now there are few satisfactions so gratifying and few annoyances so distressing as the approval and the disapproval of our comrades. Anticipated approval will care for most cases; but the positive social disapproval of one's fellows has peculiar potency. When the teacher merely coerces and the other pupils side with their comrade, a contrary 'set'—such as we earlier discussed—is almost inevitable, often so definite as to prevent the fixing in the child's character of the desired response. Conformity may be but outward. But when all concerned take part in deciding what is just—if the teacher act wisely—there is far less likelihood of an opposing 'set'. Somehow disapproval by those who understand from one's own point of view tends to dissolve an opposing 'set', and one acts then more fully from his own decision. In such cases the desired bond is better built in one's moral character. Conformity is not merely outward. It is necessary to emphasize the part the teacher plays in this group building of bonds. Left alone, as 'the gentleman's grade' in college indicates, pupils may develop habits of dawdling. Against this purposelessness the present thesis is especially directed; but proper ideals must be built up in the school group. As an ideal is but an idea joined with tendencies to act, the procedure for building has been discussed; but the teacher is responsible for the results. The pupils working under his guidance must through the social experiences encountered build the ideals necessary for approved social life. The régime of purposeful activity offers then a wider variety of educative moral experiences more nearly typical of life itself than does our usual school procedure, lends itself better to the educative evaluation of these, and provides better for the fixing of all as permanent acquisitions in the intelligent moral character.

The question of the growth or building of interests is important in the theory of the plan here discussed. Many points still prove difficult, but some things can be said. Most obvious is the fact of 'maturing' (itself a difficult topic). At first an infant responds automatically to his environment. Only later, after many experiences have been organized, can he, properly speaking, entertain purposes; and in this there are many gradations. Similarly, the earliest steps involved in working out a 'set' are those that have been instinctively joined with the process. Later on, steps may be taken by 'suggestion' (the relatively automatic working of acquired associations). Only comparatively late do we find true adaptation of means to end, the conscious choice of steps to the attainment of deliberately formed purposes. These considerations must qualify any statements made regarding child purposes. One result of the growth here discussed is the 'leading on' it affords. A skill acquired as end can be applied as means to new purposes. Skill or idea arising first in connection with means may be singled out for special consideration and so form new ends. This last is one of the most fruitful sources of new interests, particularly of the intellectual kind.

In connection with this 'maturing' goes a general increase in the 'interest span', the length of time during which a set will remain active, the time within which a child will—if allowed—work at any given project. What part of this increase is due to nature and physical maturing, what part to nurture, why the span is long for some activities and short for others, how we can increase the span in any given cases, are questions of the greatest moment for the educator. It is a matter of common knowledge that within limits 'interests' may be built up, the correlative interest spans appreciably increased. Whatever else may be said, this must mean that stimulus-response bonds have been formed and this in accordance with the laws of learning. We have already seen the general part played by the factor of purpose in utilizing the laws of learning. There seems no reason to doubt that like considerations hold here. In particular the discussion of coercion with its two opposed sets holds almost unchanged. Since the 'set' of external origin has its correlative goal and its consequent possible success, there is a theoretical possibility of learning. In this way we may conceive a new interest built by coercion. Two factors, however, greatly affect the practical utilization of this possibility, the one inherently to hinder, the other possibly to help. The inherent hindrance is the opposed (internal) set, which in proportion to its intensity and persistence will confuse the definition of success and lessen the satisfaction of attainment. Acquiring a new interest is in this respect accordingly doubly and inherently hindered by coercion. The second factor, which may act favorably, is the possibility that what (reduced learning) takes place may connect with some already potentially existent interest[1] giving such expression to it that the inner opposition to the enforced activity is won over, and the opposing set dissolved. This second factor is of especial significance for the light it throws upon the relation of teacher and pupils in this matter of coercion. It seems from these considerations that if compulsion will result in such learning as sets free some self-continuing activity and this before harmful concomitants have been set up, we may approve such compulsion as a useful temporary device. Otherwise, so far as concerns the building of interests, the use of coercion seems a choice of evils with the general probabilities opposing.[2]

It may be well to come closer to the customary subject matter of the school. Let us consider the classification of the different types of projects: Type 1, where the purpose is to embody some idea or plan in external form, as building a boat, writing a letter, presenting a play; type 2, where the purpose is to enjoy some (esthetic) experience, as listening to a story, hearing a symphony, appreciating a picture; type 3, where the purpose is to straighten out some intellectual difficulty, to solve some problem, as to find out whether or not dew falls, to ascertain how New York outgrew Philadelphia; type 4, where the purpose is to obtain some item or degree of skill or knowledge, as learning to write grade 14 on the Thorndike Scale, learning the irregular verbs in French. It is at once evident that these groupings more or less overlap and that one type may be used as means to another as end. It may be of interest to note that with these definitions the project method logically includes the problem method as a special case. The value of such a classification as that here given seems to me to lie in the light it should throw on the kind of proj-

[1] "The truth is, that, having native capacity for performing certain acts and dealing with certain classes of material, we are interested in performing these acts and handling this material; and that once these activities are aroused, they furnish their own drive. This applies to abilities developed through training as well as to strictly native capacities. Almost anything may be made play and furnish its own motive."—Woodworth, *Dynamic Psychology*, p. 202; see also pp. 59*f*., 75*f*., 102, 104, 200*f*.

[2] Coercion may be permissible as a particular expedient in some other instances, as when damage is about to be done either to others or to property or to the child himself. Clearly this is a temporary device and, even in these cases, generally a choice of evils.

There are some who needlessly confuse coercion with purposeful action in the face of difficulty. A certain stress of difficulty is healthy, probably necessary to wholeheartedness. Without it there is likely mere routine action of functions already learned. On the other hand, too great a difficulty means failure often with discouragement. In between these extremes lies the most educative activity.

ects teachers may expect and on the procedure that normally prevails in the several types. For type 1 the following steps have been suggested: purposing, planning, executing, and judging. It is in accord with the general theory here advocated that the child as far as possible take each step himself. Total failure, however, may hurt more than assistance. The opposed dangers seem to be on the one hand that the child may not come out master of the process, on the other, that he may waste time. The teacher must steer the child through these narrows, taking care meanwhile to avoid the other dangers previously discussed. The function of the purpose and the place of thinking in the process need but be mentioned. Attention may be called to the fourth step, that the child as he grows older may increasingly judge the result in terms of the aim and with increasing care and success draw from the process its lessons for the future.

Type 2, enjoying an esthetic experience, may seem to some hardly to belong in the list of projects. But the factor of purpose undoubtedly guides the process and—I must think—influences the growth of appreciation. I have, however, as yet no definite procedure steps to point out.

Type 3, that of the problem, is of all the best known, owing to the work of Professors Dewey and McMurry. The steps that have been used are those of the Dewey analysis of thought.[1] The type lends itself, next to type 4, best of all to our ordinary school-room work. For this reason I have myself feared its over-emphasis. Our schools—at least in my judgment—do emphatically need a great increase in the social activity possible in type 1. Type 4, where the purpose has to do with specific items of knowledge or skill, would seem to call for the same steps as type 1,—purposing, planning, executing, and judging. Only here, the planning had perhaps best come from the psychologist. In this type also there is danger of over-emphasis. Some teachers indeed may not closely discriminate between drill as a project and a drill as a set task, although the results will be markedly different.

The limits of the article forbid a discussion of other important aspects of the topic: the changes necessitated by this plan in room furniture and equipment, perhaps in school architecture,

[1] Dewey, *How We Think*, Chap. VI.

the new type of text-book, the new kind of curriculum and program, possibly new plans of grading and promotion, most of all, a changed attitude as to what to wish for in the way of achievement. Nor can we consider what this type of procedure means for democracy in furnishing us better citizens, alert, able to think and act, too intelligently critical to be easily hoodwinked either by politicians or by patent-medicines, self-reliant, ready of adaptation to the new social conditions that impend. The question of difficulties would itself require a separate article: opposition of tradition, of taxpayers; unprepared and incompetent teachers; the absence of a worked-out procedure; problems of administration and supervision. All these and more would suffice to destroy the movement were it not deeply grounded.

In conclusion, then, we may say that the child is naturally active, especially along social lines. Heretofore a régime of coercion has only too often reduced our schools to aimless dawdling and our pupils to selfish individualists. Some in reaction have resorted to foolish humoring of childish whims. The contention of this paper is that wholehearted purposeful activity in a social situation as the typical unit of school procedure is the best guarantee of the utilization of the child's native capacities now too frequently wasted. Under proper guidance purpose means efficiency, not only in reaching the projected end of the activity immediately at hand, but even more in securing from the activity the learning which it potentially contains. Learning of all kinds and in its all desirable ramifications best proceeds in proportion as wholeheartedness of purpose is present. With the child naturally social and with the skillful teacher to stimulate and guide his purposing, we can especially expect that kind of learning we call character building. The necessary reconstruction consequent upon these considerations offers a most alluring 'project' to the teacher who but dares to purpose.

CPSIA information can be obtained
at www.ICGtesting.com
Printed in the USA
BVHW010656270521
607867BV00021B/1267

9 781169 410480